THE FREEDOM BUSINESS

THE Freedom Business

INCLUDING
*A Narrative of the
Life & Adventures of Venture,
a Native of Africa*

POEMS BY
Marilyn Nelson
ART BY
Deborah Dancy

WORDSONG
Honesdale, Pennsylvania

To Laura Harrington, who loved the arts
—M.N.

*In memory of my mother, Evelyn Dancy,
who loved poetry, and my father,
William Dancy, who loved history*
—D.D.

Text copyright © 2008 by Marilyn Nelson
Illustrations copyright © 2008 by Deborah Dancy
All rights reserved
Printed in China
Designed by Helen Robinson
First edition

LIBRARY OF CONGRESS CATALOGING-IN-PUBLICATION DATA
Nelson, Marilyn.
The freedom business / poems by Marilyn Nelson ; art by Deborah Dancy ;
including A narrative of the life and adventures of Venture, a native of Africa.
p. cm.
ISBN 978-1-932425-57-4 (hardcover: alk. paper)
1. Smith, Venture, 1729?–1805—Poetry.
2. Slaves—Connecticut—Middle Haddam—Poetry.
3. African Americans—Connecticut—Poetry.
4. Connecticut—Poetry. 5. Smith, Venture, 1729?–1805—Juvenile literature.
6. Slavery—Connecticut—Juvenile literature.
I. Dancy, Deborah. II. Smith, Venture, 1729?–1805.
Narrative of the life and adventures of Venture, a native of Africa. III. Title.
PS3573.A4795F74 2008
811'.54—dc22
2008004437

WORDSONG
An Imprint of Boyds Mills Press, Inc.
815 Church Street
Honesdale, Pennsylvania 18431

THE FREEDOM BUSINESS

A

NARRATIVE

OF THE

LIFE AND ADVENTURES

OF

VENTURE,

A NATIVE OF AFRICA:

But resident above sixty years in the United States of America.

RELATED BY HIMSELF.

New-London:
PRINTED BY C. HOLT, AT THE BEE-OFFICE.
1798.

THE FREEDOM·BUSINESS

Marilyn Nelson

Preface

The following account of the life of VENTURE,
is a relation of simple facts, in which nothing is added
in substance to what he related himself.

Many other interesting and curious passages of his life might
have been inserted; but on account of the bulk to which they
must necessarily have swelled this narrative, they were omit-
ted. If any should suspect the truth of what is here related,
they are referred to people now living who are acquainted
with most of the facts mentioned in the narrative.

The reader is here presented with an account, not of
a renowned politician or warrior, but of an untutored
African slave, brought into this Christian country at eight
years of age, wholly destitute of all education but what he
received in common with other domesticated animals,
enjoying no advantages that could lead him to suppose
himself superior to the beasts, his fellow servants. And if
he shall derive no other advantage from perusing this narrative, he may experience those sensations of shame and
indignation, that will prove him to be not wholly destitute
of every noble and generous feeling.

Preface to the Poems

I have read many slave narratives but never one describing such victory over apparently impossible odds as Venture Smith's. He was a man caught up in a nightmare of history who nevertheless managed to retain his fundamental decency, humanity, and self-respect; a man whose inherent entrepreneurial talent outweighed his enslavement and illiteracy; a man who rose above the limitations imposed by racist economics to achieve unparalleled economic success.

I cannot pretend to have understood him at first. Venture Smith seemed very much a man of his times: an eighteenth-century rationalist for whom everything—including himself and his wife and children—had a price. I longed to see him rise above the age in which he lived, to condemn the system that put a price on his head and the heads of his people. Yet, as I worked with his story and his words, I came to understand and respect his necessities.

Venture Smith, or Broteer Furro, as he was named at birth, survived and surmounted so much. While his is a story of triumph, it also sheds light on his enslaved and free contemporaries, allowing us to glimpse their heartache, their struggle, and their interior lives. His story spoke to me across the gap of time; I responded in the poems you are about to read. I hope our words will speak to you and fill you with the courage needed to hold faith, as Venture Smith did, in our common humanity, and to stand with him against the forces of spiritual blindness and cruelty.

—*Marilyn Nelson*

The subject of the following pages, had he received only a common education, might have been a man of high respectability and usefulness; and had his education been suited to his genius, he might have been an ornament and an honor to human nature. It may perhaps, not be unpleasing to see the efforts of a great mind wholly uncultivated, enfeebled and depressed by slavery, and struggling under every disadvantage.—

The reader may here see a Franklin and a Washington, in a state of nature, or rather in a state of slavery. Destitute as he is of all education, and broken by hardships and infirmities of age, he still exhibits striking traces of native ingenuity and good sense.

This narrative exhibits a pattern of honesty, prudence and industry, to people of his own colour; and perhaps some white people would not find themselves degraded by imitating such an example.

The following account is published in compliance with the earnest desire of the subject of it, and likewise a number of respectable persons who are acquainted with him.

List of Poems

Chapter 1

Containing an account of his life, from his birth
to the time of his leaving his native country.

I WAS born at Dukandarra, in Guinea, about the year
1729. My father's name was Saungm Furro, Prince of the
Tribe of Dukandarra. My father had three wives. Polygamy
was not uncommon in that country, especially among the
rich, as every man was allowed to keep as many wives as he
could maintain. By his first wife he had three children.
The eldest of them was myself, named by my father, Broteer. The other two were named Cundazo and Soozaduka.
My father had two children by his second wife, and one
by his third. I descended from a very large, tall and stout
race of beings, much larger than the generality of people
in other parts of the globe, being commonly considerable
above six feet in height, and every way well proportioned.

The first thing worthy of notice which I remember was,
a contention between my father and mother, on account of
my father's marrying his third wife without the consent of
his first and eldest, which was contrary to the custom gen-
erally observed among my countrymen. In consequence
of this rupture, my mother left her husband and country,
and travelled away with her three children to the eastward.
I was then five years old. She took not the least sustenance
along with her, to support either herself or children. I was
able to travel along by her side; the other two of her off-
spring she carried one on her back, and the other being
a sucking child, in her arms. When we became hungry,

Witness

"My Father Named Me Broteer"

I was the first wife's firstborn of the Prince
of Dukandarra. My father was wise and strong,
a just and moderate ruler, a true king.
His name—Saungm Furro—was his only bond.
When he stood in a crowd of countrymen
(each taller, broader across shoulders and chest
than your average white man, and mahogany brown),
my father towered over most of the rest,
draped in his elegant toga of kente cloth.
When he sat, he sat on The Golden Stool.
I still remember his rumbling voice, his laugh.

(Hidden with my mother in the bushes,
      I would see him killed.)

my mother used to set us down on the ground, and gather some of the fruits which grew spontaneously in that climate. These served us for food on the way. At night we all lay down together in the most secure place we could find, and reposed ourselves until morning. Though there were many noxious animals there; yet so kind was our Almighty protector, that none of them were ever permitted to hurt or molest us. Thus we went on our journey until the second day after our departure from Dukandarra, when we came to the entrance of a great desert. During our travel in that we were often affrighted with the doleful howlings and yellings of wolves, lions, and other animals. After five days travel we came to the end of this desert, and immediately entered into a beautiful and extensive interval country. Here my mother was pleased to stop and seek a refuge for me. She left me at the house of a very rich farmer. I was then, as I should judge, not less than one hundred and forty miles from my native place, separated from all my relations and acquaintance. At this place my mother took her farewel of me, and set out for her own country. My new guardian, as I shall call the man with whom I was left, put me into the business of tending sheep, immediately after I was left with him. The flock which I kept with the assistance of a boy, consisted of about forty. We drove them every morning between two and three miles to pasture, into the wide and delightful plains. When night drew on, we drove them home and secured them in the cote. In this round I continued during my stay there. One incident which befel me when I was driving my flock from pasture, was so dreadful to me in that age, and is to this time so fresh in my memory, that I cannot help noticing it in this place. Two large dogs sallied out of a certain house and set upon me. One of

Earliest Memory

(ca. 1735)

Among the Dukandarra any man
who can afford to marries many wives.
Each wife has her own house and her own land,
and honor. A man marries first for love,
then for desire, or to beget sons.
By custom, the first wife has to approve
of the co-wives, who will learn their husband's snore,
his taste for spices. They will be co-wives for life.

Rashly, my father married a glowing, black
sixteen-year-old girl. When the news broke at home,
with her infant tied in front and her lap child on her back,
my mother took my hand and walked toward the morning sun.
We walked and walked and walked and walked and walked.
When we were hungry my mother set us down
and gathered fruit. At night, under an arc
of Divine Protection, we lay down and slept on the ground,

to the uneasy music of distant roars.
At dawn my mother woke us to walk on.
Five days in the desert, then the green answer to prayers:
a vast open land as beautiful as our own.
My mother arranged to leave me in the care
of a wealthy farmer, far from my home and kin.
Then she walked away and left me standing there.
For the first time in my life, I was alone.

them took me by the arm, and the other by the thigh, and before their master could come and relieve me, they lacerated my flesh to such a degree, that the scars are very visible to the present day. My master was immediately sent for. He came and carried me home, as I was unable to go myself on account of my wounds. Nothing remarkable happened afterwards until my father sent for me to return home.

Before I dismiss this country, I must just inform my reader what I remember concerning this place. A large river runs through this country in a westerly course. The land for a great way on each side is flat and level, hedged in by a considerable rise of the country at a great distance from it. It scarce ever rains there, yet the land is fertile; great dews fall in the night which refresh the soil. About the latter end of June or first of July, the river begins to rise, and gradually increases until it has inundated the country for a great distance, to the height of seven or eight feet. This brings on a slime which enriches the land surprisingly. When the river has subsided, the natives begin to sow and plant, and the vegetation is exceeding rapid. Near this rich river my guardian's land lay. He possessed, I cannot exactly tell how much, yet this I am certain of respecting it, that he owned an immense tract. He possessed likewise a great many cattle and goats. During my stay with him I was kindly used, and with as much tenderness, for what I saw, as his only son, although I was an entire stranger to him, remote from friends and relations. The principal occupations of the inhabitants there, were the cultivation of the soil and the care of their flocks. They were a people pretty similar in every respect to that of mine, except in their persons, which were not so tall and stout. They appeared to be very kind and friendly. I will now return to my departure from that place.

Hellhounds

(ca. 1736)

My guardian owned a good many cattle and goats.
He set me, with another boy, to tend his flock.
I spent most of the long days contemplating fate.
Nothing remarkable happened. I seldom spoke.
There were forty goats. We drove them out at dawn,
drove them back and secured them in their cotes at dusk.
The moon and nothing else changed, although I asked,
begged, bargained, offered everything I would ever own
if some Power or Powers would just change everything back.
But the silence I heard beyond the sky said no.
Nothing remarkable happened. Nothing much,
except the dog attack.

It was evening. I had almost reached home with my flock
when a pack of mongrels appeared, ears back, growls low
in their deep chests. Teeth bared, they circled, watched
for an opening. Suddenly, one of the curs
sank teeth into my thigh, and another
caught my forearm when he leaped at my throat.
Never were the Powers and my father more remote
than when, screaming, I fought back without hope.
Then my guardian beat away the dogs.
I bear outward and inward scars from my narrow escape
from those hellhounds.

My father sent a man and horse after me. After settling with my guardian for keeping me, he took me away and went for home. It was then about one year since my mother brought me here. Nothing remarkable occured to us on our journey until we arrived safe home.

I found then that the difference between my parents had been made up previous to their sending for me. On my return, I was received both by my father and mother with great joy and affection, and was once more restored to my paternal dwelling in peace and happiness. I was then about six years old.

Not more than six weeks had passed after my return, before a message was brought by an inhabitant of the place where I lived the preceding year to my father, that that place had been invaded by a numerous army, from a nation not far distant, furnished with musical instruments, and all kinds of arms then in use; that they were instigated by some white nation who equipped and sent them to subdue and possess the country; that his nation had made no preparation for war, having been for a long time in profound peace that they could not defend themselves against such a formidable train of invaders, and must therefore necessarily evacuate their lands to the fierce enemy, and fly to the protection of some chief; and that if he would permit them they should come under his rule and protection when they had to retreat from their own possessions. He was a kind and merciful prince, and therefore consented to these proposals.

He had scarcely returned to his nation with the message, before the whole of his people were obliged to retreat from their country, and come to my father's dominions.

He gave them every privilege and all the protection his government could afford. But they had not been there

Forty-two Perfect Days

(ca. 1737)

My father sent a man for me.
Engulfed again in my family
(I saw my parents openly kiss!)
I had six weeks of perfect bliss.

Six weeks of bliss, in a whole life.
And all the rest a chart of grief
islanded here and there with joys.
Like an infection which destroys
a flower beautiful and rare,
an invading army, with powdered hair,
with trumpets, muskets, and glass beads,
with lace cuffs, rum, with new-grown greeds;
like a wave of fire, like a wind all flame,
like a plague of locusts: the slavers came.

fig.

longer than four days before news came to them that the invaders had laid waste their country, and were coming speedily to destroy them in my father's territories. This affrighted them, and therefore they immediately pushed off to the southward, into the unknown countries there, and were never more heard of.

Two days after their retreat, the report turned out to be but too true. A detachment from the enemy came to my father and informed him, that the whole army was encamped not far out of his dominions, and would invade the territory and deprive his people of their liberties and rights, if he did not comply with the following terms. These were to pay them a large sum of money, three hundred fat cattle, and a great number of goats, sheep, asses, &c.

My father told the messenger he would comply rather than that his subjects should be deprived of their rights and privileges, which he was not then in circumstances to defend from so sudden an invasion. Upon turning out those articles, the enemy pledged their faith and honor that they would not attack him. On these he relied and therefore thought it unnecessary to be on his guard against the enemy. But their pledges of faith and honor proved no better than those of other unprincipled hostile nations; for a few days after a certain relation of the king came and informed him, that the enemy who sent terms of accommodation to him and received tribute to their satisfaction, yet meditated an attack upon his subjects by surprise, and that probably they would commence their attack in less than one day, and concluded with advising him, as he was not prepared for war, to order a speedy retreat of his family and subjects. He complied with this advice.

Honor among Slavers

Our captors offered my father a generous deal:
his and his people's freedom for a sum
of livestock and money.
       We were for sale.
And my father bought us.
         (Oh, what odium
those spit dogs, those foulers of human blood!)

A few days later we were forced to flee
past planted fields, to the boundary of the wild—
my father with my two little brothers, my mother with me.

Our purchased freedom had turned out to be a lie.
Around us were flames, smoke, musket fire, and the screams
of the people my father had been told he could buy.
(Accept no pledge from a man who knows no shame.)

They were priced. Those who were worthless were killed,
the others chained in coffle, to be sold.

The same night which was fixed upon to retreat, my father and his family set off about break of day. The king and his two younger wives went in one company, and my mother and her children in another. We left our dwellings in succession, and my father's company went on first. We directed our course for a large shrub plain, some distance off, where we intended to conceal ourselves from the approaching enemy, until we could refresh and rest ourselves a little. But we presently found that our retreat was not secure. For having struck up a little fire for the purpose of cooking victuals, the enemy who happened to be encamped a little distance off, had sent out a scouting party who discovered us by the smoke of the fire, just as we were extinguishing it, and about to eat. As soon as we had finished eating, my father discovered the party, and immediately began to discharge arrows at them. This was what I first saw, and it alarmed both me and the women, who being unable to make any resistance, immediately betook ourselves to the tall thick reeds not far off, and left the old king to fight alone. For some time I beheld him from the reeds defending himself with great courage and firmness, till at last he was obliged to surrender himself into their hands.

They then came to us in the reeds, and the very first salute I had from them was a violent blow on the head with the fore part of a gun, and at the same time a grasp round the neck. I then had a rope put about my neck, as had all the women in the thicket with me, and were immediately led to my father, who was likewise pinioned and haltered for leading. In this condition we were all led to the camp. The women and myself being pretty submissive, had tolerable treatment from the enemy, while my father was closely

A Treasure Buried

My father fought on alone, against a future
where a king's children's children would be slaves,
valuables exchanged for filthy lucre
to line the pockets of black and white thieves.

The thieves demanded my father's royal treasure.
(I had helped him bury it in a shallow grave
that night: cowries, carved masks of Ancestors,
The Golden Stool. ...) My father refused to save
his life at the price of Dukandarra's honor.
Beaten with fists and gunstocks, cut with knives
by men who grinned as they inflicted torture,
dying, he was as noble as he was alive.
In every way, here was a remarkable man.
Sometimes, remembering, I am overcome.

interrogated respecting his money which they knew he must have. But as he gave them no account of it, he was instantly cut and pounded on his body with great inhumanity, that he might be induced by the torture he suffered to make the discovery. All this availed not in the least to make him give up his money, but he despised all the tortures which they inflicted, until the continued exercise and increase of torment, obliged him to sink and expire.

He thus died without informing his enemies of the place where his money lay. I saw him while he was thus tortured to death. The shocking scene is to this day fresh in my mind, and I have often been overcome while thinking on it. He was a man of remarkable stature. I should judge as much as six feet and six or seven inches high, two feet across his shoulders, and every way well proportioned. He was a man of remarkable strength and resolution, affable, kind and gentle, ruling with equity and moderation.

The army of the enemy was large, I should suppose consisting of about six thousand men. Their leader was called Baukurre. After destroying the old prince, they decamped and immediately marched towards the sea, lying to the west, taking with them myself and the women prisoners. In the march a scouting party was detached from the main army. To the leader of this party I was made waiter, having to carry his gun, &c.—As we were a scouting we came across a herd of fat cattle, consisting of about thirty in number. These we set upon, and immediately wrested from their keepers, and afterwards converted them into food for the army. The enemy had remarkable success in destroying the country wherever they went. For as far as they had penetrated, they laid the habitations waste and captured the people. The distance they had now brought me was about

Pestilence

Six thousand men strong, the army poured toward the sea.
Slavery's wide wings gliding overhead
spread an infecting shadow as, step by step,
they swept like a battalion of ravenous ants,
advancing through the landscape and leaving a stench
drenched in sweat, shit, vomit, terror, and smoke.
The gentlefolk of every village burned,
borne by the black tide, shuffled in the slavers' wake,
awake for the first time to a larger fate,
indeterminate but nasty: on the world stage
in an age when a workforce could be bought and sold.
Golden, the flow of human life down the green slopes.
Hopes shriveled in the glare of the distant bright
whitewashed castle's acrid glitter in sunlight.

four hundred miles. All the march I had very hard tasks imposed on me, which I must perform on pain of punishment. I was obliged to carry on my head a large flat stone used for grinding our corn, weighing as I should suppose, as much as 25 pounds; besides victuals, mat and cooking utensils. Though I was pretty large and stout of my age, yet these burthens were very grievous to me, being only about six years and an half old.

We were then come to a place called Malagasco.—When we entered the place we could not see the least appearance of either houses or inhabitants, but upon stricter search found, that instead of houses above ground they had dens in the sides of hillocks, contiguous to ponds and streams of water. In these we perceived they had all hid themselves, as I suppose they usually did upon such occasions. In order to compel them to surrender, the enemy contrived to smoke them out with faggots. These they put to the entrance of the caves and set them on fire. While they were engaged in this business, to their great surprise some of them were desperately wounded with arrows which fell from above on them. This mystery they soon found out. They perceived that the enemy discharged these arrows through holes on the top of the dens directly into the air.—Their weight brought them back, point downwards on their enemies heads, whilst they were smoking the inhabitants out. The points of their arrows were poisoned, but their enemy had an antidote for it, which they instantly applied to the wounded part. The smoke at last obliged the people to give themselves up. They came out of their caves, first spatting the palms of their hands together, and immediately after extended their arms, crossed at their wrists, ready to be bound and pinioned. I should judge that the dens above mentioned were extended

Anamaboo

The black tide fell on the people of Anamaboo,
who, seeing slaves and slavers, knew what to do:
you wait for an opening. ... The slavers were tired.
Fired up—still and already—on rum,
some of them walked as though they were asleep.
Agape, the slaves watched the Anamabooites
fight brilliantly against their enemy.
With glee the slaves cheered them toward victory
and jubilee. Instead of freeing them, the Anamaboon
opportunists captured their slavers. Tied
beside people they had captured in their own harsh
march, like them the enslaved slavers wept,
swept toward the coast by grinning Anamaboo,
who would be sold by their neighbors, in a month or two.

about eight feet horizontally into the earth, six feet in height and as many wide. They were arched over head and lined with earth, which was of the clay kind, and made the surface of their walls firm and smooth.

The invaders then pinioned the prisoners of all ages and sexes indiscriminately, took their flocks and all their effects, and moved on their way towards the sea. On the march the prisoners were treated with clemency, on account of their being submissive and humble. Having come to the next tribe, the enemy laid siege and immediately took men, women, children, flocks, and all their valuable effects. They then went on to the next district which was contiguous to the sea, called in Africa, Anamaboo. The enemies provisions were then almost spent, as well as their strength. The inhabitants knowing what conduct they had pursued, and what were their present intentions, improved the favorable opportunity, attacked them, and took enemy, prisoners; flocks and all their effects. I was then taken a second time. All of us were then put into the castle, and kept for market. On a certain time I and other prisoners were put on board a canoe, under our master, and rowed away to a vessel belonging to Rhode-Island, commanded by capt. Collingwood, and the mate Thomas Mumford. While we were going to the vessel, our master told us all to appear to the best possible advantage for sale. I was bought on board by one Robertson Mumford, steward of said vessel, for four gallons of rum, and a piece of calico, and called VENTURE, on account of his having purchased me with his own private venture. Thus I came by my name. All the slaves that were bought for that vessel's cargo, were two hundred and sixty.

How I Came By My Name

Four casks of rum and a bolt of calico.
(A quarter of the list price. A terrific deal,
a steal for the ship's steward who bought a boy
onboard as two-legged cargo was being loaded
and stowed.) Four casks of rum and a piece of cloth.
(For breath, dreams, heartbeat.) The boy who was Broteer
disappeared. A business venture took his place.
Same face, same eyes, but inside utterly transformed,
harmed past healing by the cheapening of human life.
Breath, dreams, pulse, traded for cloth and alcohol,
were *capital*. There was *profit* in the pain,
the chains. *Venture*. There were whole worlds to gain.

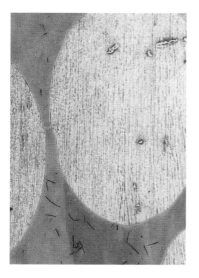

Chapter 2

AFTER all the business was ended on the coast of Africa,
the ship sailed from thence to Barbadoes. After an ordinary passage, except great mortality by the small pox, which
broke out on board, we arrived at the island of Barbadoes:
but when we reached it, there were found out of the two
hundred and sixty that sailed from Africa, not more than
two hundred alive. These were all sold, except myself and
three more, to the planters there.

The vessel then sailed for Rhode-Island, and arrived
there after a comfortable passage. Here my master sent me
to live with one of his sisters, until he could carry me to
Fisher's Island, the place of his residence. I had then completed my eighth year. After staying with his sister some
time I was taken to my master's place to live.

When we arrived at Narraganset, my master went ashore
in order to return a part of the way by land, and gave me
the charge of the keys of his trunks on board the vessel,
and charged me not to deliver them up to any body, not
even to his father without his orders. To his directions I
promised faithfully to conform. When I arrived with my
master's articles at his house, my master's father asked me
for his son's keys, as he wanted to see what his trunks con-
tained. I told him that my master intrusted me with the
care of them until he should return, and that I had given
him my word to be faithful to the trust, and could not

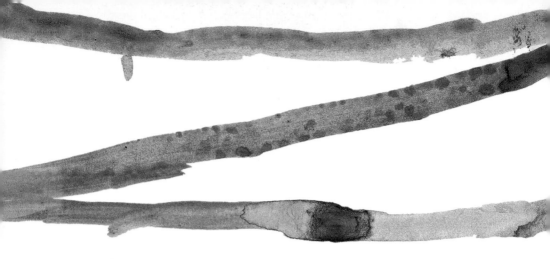

A Voyage by Sea
(1738)

Eleven months on the *Charming Susanna*.
"An ordinary passage." But smallpox
amok in the hold set sixty people free.
The sea gulped them down in a boil of grins and fins,
men and women tossed like offal to the sharks.

Discharge excretion diarrhea spew
oozing pustular nausea vomit snot

Brought from Africa, they were to be sold to the New World
as fuel for the grinding machines of history.

Festering sticky shit-smeared mucus pus
pissed-on menstruating sweaty stinking

                  Dazed
and erased en route before they were renamed
by whim, who were those anonymous, generic slaves,
graveless as garbage, splashed to the greedy waves?

therefore give him or any other person the keys without my master's directions. He insisted that I should deliver to him the keys, threatening to punish me if I did not. But I let him know that he should not have them let him say what he would. He then laid aside trying to get them. But notwithstanding he appeared to give up trying to obtain them from me, yet I mistrusted that he would take some time when I was off my guard, either in the day time or at night to get them, therefore I slung them round my neck, and in the day time concealed them in my bosom, and at night I always lay with them under me, that no person might take them from me without being apprized of it. Thus I kept the keys from every body until my master came home. When he returned he asked where VENTURE was. As I was then within hearing, I came, and said, here sir, at your service. He asked me for his keys, and I immediately took them off my neck and reached them out to him. He took them, stroked my hair, and commended me, saying in presence of his father that his young VENTURE was so faithful that he never would have been able to have taken the keys from him but by violence; that he should not fear to trust him with his whole fortune, for that he had been in his native place so habituated to keeping his word, that he would sacrifice even his life to maintain it.

The first of the time of living at my master's own place, I was pretty much employed in the house at carding wool and other houshold business. In this situation I continued for some years, after which my master put me to work out of doors. After many proofs of my faithfulness and honesty, my master began to put great confidence in me. My behavior to him had as yet been submissive and obedient. I then began to have hard tasks imposed on me. Some of

Keeper of the Keys
(1740)

What makes a man a man is his good name:
the rest of it is beyond our control.
Trustworthiness and honor are riches
no one can steal. Let men have faith in you;
hold true to your promise. My father's values
were my sum and substance during that cocoon year.

From freedom to a new world was one year
of grief, shock, sorrow, and learning my new name
and Master's language. But not Master's values:
here, at least, was something I could control.
Here, there was a true, essential *I*
which only I could own. Here were my riches.

In Barbados, the surviving unpurchased riches
were barbered, washed, and oiled. After a year
of misery and homeward yearning, they
were marched to market, sold, and given new names,
their present strength and their futures under white control,
their traditional beliefs toppled under Christian values.

I was nine years old, and filled with my father's values,
when we reached Rhode Island. From there my master's riches
sailed to his home, his keys under my control,
while he disembarked for business. For a year
I had practiced *Become True Virtue. Bring Honor to Your Name.*
Now I promised my master his keys would be safe with me.

these were to pound four bushels of ears of corn every night in a barrel for the poultry, or be rigorously punished. At other seasons of the year I had to card wool until a very late hour. These tasks I had to perform when I was about nine years old. Some time after I had another difficulty and oppression which was greater than any I had ever experienced since I came into this country. This was to serve two masters. James Mumford, my master's son, when his father had gone from home in the morning, and given me a stint to perform that day, would order me to do *this* and *that* business different from what my master directed me. One day in particular, the authority which my master's son had set up, had like to have produced melancholy effects. For my master having set me off my business to perform that day and then left me to perform it, his son came up to me in the course of the day, big with authority, and commanded me very arrogantly to quit my present business and go directly about what he should order me. I replied to him that my master had given me so much to perform that day, and that I must therefore faithfully complete it in that time. He then broke out into a great rage, snatched a pitchfork and went to lay me over the head therewith; but I as soon got another and defended myself with it, or otherwise be might have murdered me in his outrage. He immediately called some people who were within hearing at work for him, and ordered them to take his hair rope and come and bind me with it. They all tried to bind me but in vain, tho' there were three assistants in number. My upstart master then desisted, put his pocket handkerchief before his eyes and went home with a design to tell his mother of the struggle with young VENTURE. He told her that their young VENTURE had become so stubborn that he could not controul him, and asked her what he should do with

At Master's home, his father ordered me
to give him the keys, as there were some things of value
among Master's things, which were purchased in his name.
I told him my master had trusted me with his riches;
I had promised to keep them safe. After a year
of becoming, I emerged. I took control.

My master's father threatened, but I controlled
the keys, concealed in my shirt, or under me
while I slept, more watchfully than I'd slept all year.
When at last my master unpacked his things of value,
he told his father he would trust me with all of his riches,
because, where I come from, a man is as good as his name.

What value has a man, beyond his name?
Can he control his fate? Know his death year?
He is richest whose honor outlives him.

him. In the mean time I recovered my temper, voluntarily caused myself to be bound by the same men who tried in vain before, and carried before my young master, that he might do what he pleased with me. He took me to a gallows made for the purpose of hanging cattle on, and suspended me on it. Afterwards he ordered one of his hands to go to the peach orchard and cut him three dozen of whips to punish me with. These were brought to him, and that was all that was done with them, as I was released and went to work after hanging on the gallows about an hour.

After I had lived with my master thirteen years, being then about twenty two years old, I married Meg, a slave of his who was about my age. My master owned a certain Irishman, named Heddy, who about that time formed a plan of secretly leaving his master. After he had long had this plan in meditation he suggested it to me. At first I cast a deaf ear to it, and rebuked Heddy for harboring in his mind such a rash undertaking. But after he had persuaded and much enchanted me with the prospect of gaining my freedom by such a method, I at length agreed to accompany him. Heddy next inveigled two of his fellow servants to accompany us. The place to which we designed to go was the Mississippi. Our next business was to lay in a sufficient store of provisions for our voyage. We privately collected out of our master's store, six great old cheeses, two firkins of butter, and one whole batch of new bread. When we had gathered all our own clothes and some more, we took them all about midnight, and went to the water side. We stole our master's boat, embarked, and then directed our course for the Mississippi river.

We mutually confederated not to betray or desert one another on pain of death. We first steered our course for

Two Masters

(ca. 1750)

For the first few years of living with my master
I was pretty much involved with household business—
fetching things, carding wool. Thus I went on,
submissive and obedient, following orders
every day with faithfulness and honesty,
earning my master's complete confidence.

As I grew taller and stronger, his confidence
in me set harder tasks for me to master,
as if he would measure the depth of my faithfulness.
Of course, I had no say in this business,
my business being to do as I was ordered,
to be the beast pulling Master's family on.

One morning, Master had given me a task and gone
away for the day. Swaggering with confidence,
his peach-cheeked son gave me a contrary order.
I told him I'd promised to complete a job for my master.
I had no right to refuse his enterprise,
he yelled, in his eyes no spark of charity.

He snatched a pitchfork. I weighed *fight* against *faith*
for one moment, then snatched the other one.
We faced off like devils going about their business,
he big with arrogance, claiming authority,
I defending my promise to my master,
and Master's confidence that I would fulfill his orders.

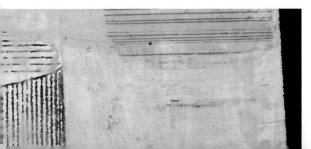

Montauk point, the east end of Long-Island. After our arrival there we landed, and Heddy and I made an incursion into the island after fresh water, while our two comrades were left at a little distance from the boat, employed at cooking. When Heddy and I had sought some time for water, he returned to our companions, and I continued on looking for my object. When Heddy had performed his business with our companions who were engaged in cooking, he went directly to the boat, stole all the clothes in it, and then travelled away for East-Hampton, as I was informed. I returned to my fellows not long after. They informed me that our clothes were stolen, but could not determine who was the thief, yet they suspected Heddy as he was missing. After reproving my two comrades for not taking care of our things which were in the boat, I advertised Heddy and sent two men in search of him. They pursued and overtook him at Southampton and returned him to the boat. I then thought it might afford some chance for my freedom, or at least a palliation for my running away, to return Heddy immediately to his master, and inform him that I was induced to go away by Heddy's address. Accordingly I set off with him and the rest of my companions for our master's, and arrived there without any difficulty. I informed my master that Heddy was the ringleader of our revolt, and that he had used us ill. He immediately put Heddy into custody, and myself and companions were well received and went to work as usual.

Not a long time passed after that, before Heddy was sent by my master to New-London gaol. At the close of that year I was sold to a Thomas Stanton, and had to be separated from my wife and one daughter, who was about one month old. He resided at Stonington-point. To this place

I held off three men my upstart master ordered
to tie me up. At last he gave up hope
and ran to his mother. As soon as he left I mastered
my temper and volunteered to put on
the hair-rope bond and be carried to him, confident
that he knew hurting me hurt Master's business.

He had me suspended on a gallows made for the business
of butchering cattle, and loudly gave orders
for twig whips to be cut. But he lost courage
and did no more. And the leopard-skin shield of faith
protected me while, by my wrists, I hung on
the gallows for refusing to serve two masters.

No man can be faithful to two masters.
All of life's business is centered in trust.
Even in an insane world, there must be some order.

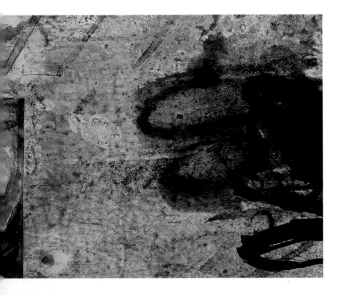

I brought with me from my late master's, two johannes, three old Spanish dollars, and two thousand of coppers, besides five pounds of my wife's money. This money I got by cleaning gentlemen's shoes and drawing boots, by catching musk-rats and minks, raising potatoes and carrots, &c. and by fishing in the night, and at odd spells.

All this money amounting to near twenty-one pounds York currency, my master's brother, Robert Stanton, hired of me, for which he gave me his note. About one year and a half after that time, my master purchased my wife and her child, for seven hundred pounds old tenor. One time my master sent me two miles after a barrel of molasses, and ordered me to carry it on my shoulders. I made out to carry it all the way to my master's house. When I lived with Captain George Mumford, only to try my strength, I took up on my knees a tierce of salt containing seven bushels, and carried it two or three rods. Of this fact there are several eye witnesses now living.

Towards the close of the time that I resided with this master, I had a falling out with my mistress. This happened one time when my master was gone to Long-Island a gunning. At first the quarrel began between my wife and her mistress. I was then at work in the barn, and hearing a racket in the house, induced me to run there and see what had broken out. When I entered the house, I found my mistress in a violent passion with my wife, for what she informed me was a mere trifle; such a small affair that I forbear to put my mistress to the shame of having it known. I earnestly requested my wife to beg pardon of her mistress for the sake of peace, even if she had given no just occasion for offence. But whilst I was thus saying my mistress turned the blows which she was repeating on my

Whispered Plans

(1754)

After my master's son hanged me by my wrists
on the cattle gallows, I decided to resist.
My master owned a certain Irishman
named Heddy, who had formed a plan
to run away. He confided his plan to me
and two other enslaved men
over a jug of poteen:
we'd steal ourselves and go west, where a man could be free.

We filched two firkins of butter, six wheels of cheese,
and a batch of bread. We bundled up our clothes
and met past midnight on the moon-dark shore.
Pushing off Master's boat, we swore
an oath of loyalty, come what might come.
We put in at Montauk first,
all of us dying of thirst:
no one had thought to bring drinking water from home.

Heddy instructed our mates to prepare a meal
whilst we sought water. After walking awhile,
he said he had something important to say
to our comrades, and walked away.
He went straight to the boat, and stole it and our clothes.
Sensing that this could be
my opportunity,
I caught and accused him of planning our revolt.

wife to me. She took down her horse-whip, and while she was glutting her fury with it, I reached out my great black hand, raised it up and received the blows of the whip on it which were designed for my head. Then I immediately committed the whip to the devouring fire.

When my master returned from the island, his wife told him of the affair, but for the present he seemed to take no notice of it, and mentioned not a word about it to me. Some days after his return, in the morning as I was putting on a log in the fire-place, not suspecting harm from any one, I received a most violent stroke on the crown of my head with a club two feet long and as large round as a chair-post. This blow very badly wounded my head, and the scar of it remains to this day. The first blow made me have my wits about me you may suppose, for as soon as he went to renew it, I snatched the club out of his hands and dragged him out of the door. He then sent for his brother to come and assist him, but I presently left my master, took the club he wounded me with, carried it to a neighboring Justice of the Peace, and complained of my master. He finally advised me to return to my master, and live contented with him till he abused me again, and then complain. I consented to do accordingly. But before I set out for my master's, up he come and his brother Robert after me. The Justice improved this convenient opportunity to caution my master. He asked him for what he treated his slave thus hastily and unjustly, and told him what would be the consequence if he continued the same treatment towards me. After the Justice had ended his discourse with my master, he and his brother set out with me for home, one before and the other behind me.

When they had come to a bye place, they both dismounted their respective horses, and fell to beating me

Heddy was jailed. At the end of the year I was sold.
Thus ended Heddy's plan to explore the world
west of the Mississippi: a paradise
he wished to see with his own eyes.
We had sailed east, in a catboat with a gaff-rigged sail,
led by a fool whose dreams
were painted-over schemes.
I should have known his plan was doomed to fail.

with great violence. I became enraged at this and immediately turned them both under me, laid one of them across the other, and stamped both with my feet what I would.

This occasioned my master's brother to advise him to put me off. A short time after this I was taken by a constable and two men. They carried me to a blacksmith's shop and had me hand-cuffed. When I returned home my mistress enquired much of her waiters, whether VENTURE was hand-cuffed. When she was informed that I was, she appeared to be very contented and was much transported with the news. In the midst of this content and joy, I presented myself before my mistress, shewed her my hand-cuffs, and gave her thanks for my gold rings. For this my master commanded a negro of his to fetch him a large ox chain. This my master locked on my legs with two padlocks. I contitinued to wear the chain peaceably for two or three days, when my master asked me with contemptuous hard names whether I had not better be freed from my chains and go to work. I answered him, No. Well then, said me, I will send you to the West-Indies or banish you, for I am resolved not to keep you. I answered him I crossed the waters to come here, and I am willing to cross them to return.

For a day or two after this not any one said much to me, until one Hempsted Miner, of Stonington, asked me if I would live with him. I answered him that I would. He then requested me to make myself discontented and to appear as unreconciled to my master as I could before that he bargained with him for me; and that in return he would give me a good chance to gain my freedom when I came to live with him. I did as he requested me. Not long after Hempsted Miner purchased me of my master for fifty-six pounds lawful. He took the chain and padlocks from off me immediately after.

44

Fat on the Fire

(ca. 1756)

I was sold to a Thomas Stanton of Stonington,
and parted from my Meg and our newborn
(our first, our Hannah). I carried a saved sum—
two thousand coppers and ten silver coins,
amounting to twenty-one pounds—rolled in my coat.
My master's brother borrowed my savings of me,
first giving me his signed I.O.U. note.
It took a year to get Master to agree
to purchase Meg and Hannah (seven hundred pounds).
Hannah's a feisty, curious little imp.
She walked at ten months; now she's running around
sticking little brown fingers into everything.

Today, a caterwaul called me from the barn
to find the source of a blood-curdling screech.
Instead of marauders bent on doing harm,
I found Mistress promising Meg she'd teach
her to let that damned pup spoil her nap.
All three of them were screaming like mad seagulls,
and Mistress was striking Meg with her horsewhip.
Now I've gone and done something that breaks all of their rules—
my master will probably sell me to the first buyer;
I might as well kiss my loaned life savings farewell—
I seized that whip and hurled it on the fire.
It sizzled like a slave-owner's soul in hell.

It may here be remembered, that I related a few pages back, that I hired out a sum of money to Mr. Robert Stanton, and took his note for it. In the fray between my master Stanton and myself, he broke open my chest containing his brother's note to me, and destroyed it. Immediately after my present master bought me, he determined to sell me at Hartford. As soon as I became apprized of it, I bethought myself that I would secure a certain sum of money which lay by me, safer than to hire it out to a Stanton. Accordingly I buried it in the earth, a little distance from Thomas Stanton's, in the road over which he passed daily. A short time after my master carried me to Hartford, and first proposed to sell me to one William Hooker of that place. Hooker asked whether I would go to the German Flats with him. I answered, No. He said I should, if not by fair means I should by foul. If you will go by no other measures, I will tie you down in my sleigh. I replied to him, that if he carried me in that manner, no person would purchase me, for it would be thought that he had a murderer for sale. After this he tried no more, and said he would not have me as a gift.

My master next offered me to Daniel Edwards, Esq. of Hartford, for sale. But not purchasing me, my master pawned me to him for ten pounds, and returned to Stonington. After some trial of my honesty, Mr. Edwards placed considerable trust and confidence in me. He put me to serve as his cup-bearer and waiter. When there was company at his house, he would send me into his cellar and other parts of his house to fetch wine and other articles occasionally for them. When I had been with him some time, he asked me why my master wished to part with such an honest negro, and why he did not keep me himself. I replied that I could not give him the reason, unless it was to convert me into cash, and speculate with me as with other

Meg

after Léopold Senghor

My love, rest your soothing hands on my brow, your fingers smooth as velvet fur.
Above us, the listing trees barely rustle in the high night's breath.
No sound of lullaby.
Let this rhythmic silence hold us.

Let us listen to its music, listen to our drumming, dark blood; listen
to the deep pulse of Africa beating in forgotten villages.
Weary, the moon gropes her way toward her bed in the sea.
Now scattered laughter grows sleepy; even the storytellers
nod like babies tied on their mothers' backs.
Now the dancers' feet grow heavy, and leaden the chorus of call and response.
This is the hour of stars and of the night, dreaming
where she lies on a hill of clouds, wrapped in a length of milky-way cloth.
The thatched roofs gleam tenderly. What do they whisper to the stars?
Inside, the fires die among familiar smells, pungent and delicious.
My love, light the lamp of clear oil, so the Ancestors may gather and talk like parents
when their children are asleep.
Let us listen to the voices of our Ancients. Like us exiled,
they do not want to die and have the river of their seed disappear into desert sands.
Let me listen, in the fading smoke, as their welcome spirits visit.
My head on your breast warm as manioc steaming from the fire,
let me breathe the scent of our Dead, remember and be their living voice,
learn from them to live
before I descend, like a coral diver,
to the soaring depths of sleep.

commodities. I hope that he can never justly say it was on account of my ill conduct that he did not keep me himself. Mr. Edwards told me that he should be very willing to keep me himself, and that he would never let me go from him to live, if it was not unreasonable and inconvenient for me to be parted from my wife and children; therefore he would furnish me with a horse to return to Stonington, if I had a mind for it. As Miner did not appear to redeem me I went, and called at my old master Stanton's first to see my wife, who was then owned by him. As my old master appeared much ruffled at my being there, I left my wife before I had spent any considerable time with her, and went to Colonel O. Smith's. Miner had not as yet wholly settled with Stanton for me, and had before my return from Hartford given Col. Smith a bill of sale of me. These men once met to determine which of them should hold me, and upon my expressing a desire to be owned by Col. Smith, and upon my master's settling the remainder of the money which was due to Stanton for me, it was agreed that I should live with Col. Smith. This was the third time of my being sold, and I was then thirty-one years old. As I never had an opportunity of redeeming myself whilst I was owned by Miner, though he promised to give me a chance, I was then very ambitious of obtaining it. I asked my master one time if he would consent to have me purchase my freedom. He replied that he would. I was then very happy, knowing that I was at that time able to pay part of the purchase money, by means of the money which I some time since buried. This I took out of the earth and tendered to my master, having previously engaged a free negro man to take his security for it, as I was the property of my master, and therefore could not safely take his obligation myself. What was

December Moonrise
(1763)

Who owns these woods basks by his hearth.
Feel like the loneliest man on earth,
sweet-talking Big Boy through these drifts.
Moonlight falls on two clouds of breath.

Patience and sweat, God-trust and thrift
might coax a curse into a gift.
Mayhap, two hundred years from now,
descendants will read my epitaph.

Me and Big Boy, the moon, the snow.
Snow thumps soft from a weighed-down bough.
My bones so weary, I could near about weep.
A hoot owl in the field below.

The money from working at night, I keep.
Saving for freedom. And I ain't cheap.
Last night I chopped wood in my sleep.
Last night I chopped wood in my sleep.

wanting in redeeming myself, my master agreed to wait on me for, until I could procure it for him. I still continued to work for Col. Smith. There was continually some interest accruing on my master's note to my friend the free negro man above named, which I received, and with some besides which I got by fishing, I laid out in land adjoining my old master Stanton's. By cultivating this land with the greatest diligence and economy, at times when my master did not require my labor, in two years I laid up ten pounds. This my friend tendered my master for myself, and received his note for it.

Being encouraged by the success which I had met in redeeming myself, I again solicited my master for a further chance of completing it. The chance for which I solicited him was that of going out to work the ensuing winter. He agreed to this on condition that I would give him one quarter of my earnings. On these terms I worked the following winter, and earned four pounds sixteen shillings, one quarter of which went to my master for the privilege, and the rest was paid him on my own account. This added to the other payments made up forty four pounds, eight shillings, which I had paid on my own account. I was then about thirty five years old.

The next summer I again desired he would give me a chance of going out to work. But he refused and answered that he must have my labor this summer, as he did not have it the past winter. I replied that I considered it as hard that I could not have a chance to work out when the season became advantageous, and that I must only be permitted to hire myself out in the poorest season of the year. He asked me after this what I would give him for the privilege per month. I replied that I would leave it wholly with

Sailing to Saybrook
(1766)

I wonder if anyone owns that little island.
It would cost only a few hours of work
to convert those trees to firewood to sell in Saybrook,
in the alchemy of silver out of sweat.
But everything has either a price or an owner,
here where dark people are commodities
to speculate on or convert to cash.
How do you buy an island? Who do you pay?
Could I hop ashore, raise a scrap of cloth as a flag,
and claim a new land, in the name of Meg?

his own generosity to determine what I should return him a month. Well then, said he, if so two pounds a month. I answered him that if that was the least he would take I would be contented.

Accordingly I hired myself out at Fisher's Island, and earned twenty pounds; thirteen pounds six shillings of which my master drew for the privilege, and the remainder I paid him for my freedom. This made fifty-one pounds two shillings which I paid him. In October following I went and wrought six months at Long Island. In that six month's time I cut and corded four hundred cords of wood, besides threshing out seventy-five bushels of grain, and received of my wages down only twenty pounds, which left remaining a larger sum. Whilst I was out that time, I took up on my wages only one pair of shoes. At night I lay on the hearth, with one coverlet over and another under me. I returned to my master and gave him what I received of my six months labor. This left only thirteen pounds eighteen shillings to make up the full sum for my redemption. My master liberated me, saying that I might pay what was behind if I could ever make it convenient, otherwise it would be well. The amount of the money which I had paid my master towards redeeming my time, was seventy-one pounds two shillings. The reason of my master for asking such an unreasonable price, was he said, to secure himself in case I should ever come to want. Being thirty-six years old, I left Col. Smith once for all. I had already been sold three different times, made considerable money with seemingly nothing to derive it from, been cheated out of a large sum of money, lost much by misfortunes, and paid an enormous sum for my freedom.

Aubade
(1768)

Started out early, following last night's track.
A moon sliver lingered over the moon blue snow.
I left my lady laying on her back
trumpeting the most beautiful music I know.
Can't take her home with me, where she belongs,
to warm my room with her smile, my pillow with her cheek.
She and our children: owned. (God must bear wrongs
like a strong black man pretending to be meek.)
Like me, my Meg was kidnapped as a child
and raised in a white home, the only slave.
We are resurrecting the portions of us killed,
inventing together a language to express love.
Sometimes we whisper words lost long ago.
I'd rather be with her now than out here
      in this god-forsaken snow.

Chapter 3

*Containing an account of his life, from the time
of his purchasing his freedom to the present day.*

MY wife and children were yet in bondage to Mr. Thomas
Stanton. About this time I lost a chest, containing besides
clothing, about thirty-eight pounds in paper money. It was
burnt by accident. A short time after I sold all my possessions at Stonington, consisting of a pretty piece of land and
one dwelling house thereon, and went to reside at Long-
Island. For the first four years of my residence there, I
spent my time in working for various people on that and
at the neighboring islands. In the space of six months I
cut and corded upwards of four hundred cords of wood.
Many other singular and wonderful labors I performed in
cutting wood there, which would not be inferior to those
just recited, but for brevity sake I must omit them. In the
aforementioned four years what wood I cut at Long-Island
amounted to several thousand cords, and the money which
I earned thereby amounted to two hundred and seven
pounds ten shillings. This money I laid up carefully by me.
Perhaps some may enquire what maintained me all the time
I was laying up money. I would inform them that I bought
nothing which I did not absolutely want. All fine clothes I
despised in comparison with my interest, and never kept
but just what clothes were comfortable for common days,
and perhaps I would have a garment or two which I did not
have on at all times, but as for superfluous finery I never
thought it to be compared with a decent homespun dress,

Work Song

I went to sea for seven months,
sing hi-ho, laddies, hi-ho,
in a whaling shop with Captain Smith,
sing hi-ho, laddies, hi-ho.

At first I was not black, but green,
sing hi-ho, laddies, hi-ho,
learning the ropes and the routine,
sing hi-ho, laddies, hi-ho.

We rendered two leviathans,
sing hi-ho, laddies, hi-ho,
to four hundred barrels of midnight sun,
sing hi-ho, laddies, hi-ho.

My pay was eighty pounds: one man.
Sing hi-ho, laddies, hi-ho.
Eighty pounds: one African.
Sing hi-ho, laddies, hi-ho.

I remembered the first time I went to sea,
sing hi-ho, laddies, hi-ho,
crammed skin to skin with misery,
sing hi-ho, laddies, hi-ho.

On nights when I drew graveyard watch,
sing hi-ho, laddies, hi-ho,
sometimes I gave in to heartache.
Sing hi-ho, laddies, hi-ho.

a good supply of money and prudence. Expensive gatherings of my mates I commonly shunned, and all kinds of luxuries I was perfectly a stranger to; and during the time I was employed in cutting the aforementioned quantity of wood, I never was at the expence of six-pence worth of spirits. Being after this labour forty years of age, I worked at various places, and in particular on Ram-Island, where I purchased Solomon and Cuff, two sons of mine, for two hundred dollars each.

It will here be remembered how much money I earned by cutting wood in four years. Besides this I had considerable money, amounting in all to near three hundred pounds. When I had purchased my two sons, I had then left more than one hundred pounds. After this I purchased a negro man, for no other reason than to oblige him, and gave for him sixty pounds. But in a short time after he run away from me, and I thereby lost all that I gave for him, except twenty pounds which he paid me previous to his absconding. The rest of my money I laid out in land, in addition to a farm which I owned before, and a dwelling house thereon. Forty four years had then completed their revolution since my entrance into this existence of servitude and misfortune. Solomon my eldest son, being then in his seventeenth year, and all my hope and dependence for help, I hired him out to one Charles Church, of Rhode-Island, for one year, on consideration of his giving him twelve pounds and an opportunity of acquiring some learning. In the course of the year, Church fitted out a vessel for a whaling voyage, and being in want of hands to man her, he induced my son to go, with the promise of giving him on his return, a pair of silver buckles, besides his wages. As soon as I heard of his going to sea, I immediately

Cows in the Shade

(1770)

Circling and circling the lazy meadow glare
the redtail sees exactly the right chance,
and life feeds life. Good afternoon, ladies,
how do you do? With your permission. Look:
just up there, on that sunny vacant spot
a Pequot village died out, of the pox.
There must be more than sixty unmarked graves
up toward the tree line. Dug a few myself.

Surely they must have thought God died. Like me,
when I was pushed onboard, my life to feed
the coffers of a stranger. Yet things fall
together again. The truth is, the earth heals
over our fates as over a taken squirrel's.
Perhaps we are not the center. Perhaps you
young ladies are Creation's best success,
chewing the cud and contemplating time
with blank-eyed innocence. Just visited
a man I shall buy and set to work for me.
I can make up my investment in six months,
even if I give him forty percent.
I'll hire him out at haying first. Good day.
Let's see: if I can talk his master down ...

set out to go and prevent it if possible.—But on my arrival at Church's, to my great grief, I could only see the vessel my son was in almost out of sight going to sea. My son died of the scurvy in this voyage, and Church has never yet paid me the least of his wages. In my son, besides the loss of his life, I lost equal to seventy-five pounds.

My other son being but a youth, still lived with me. About this time I chartered a sloop of about thirty tons burthen, and hired men to assist me in navigating her. I employed her mostly in the wood trade to Rhode-Island, and made clear of all expences above one hundred dollars with her in better than one year. I had then become something forehanded, and being in my forty-fourth year, I purchased my wife Meg, and thereby prevented having another child to buy, as she was then pregnant. I gave forty pounds for her.

During my residence at Long-Island, I raised one year with another, ten cart loads of water-melons, and lost a great many every year besides by the thievishness of the sailors. What I made by the water-melons I sold there, amounted to nearly five hundred dollars. Various other methods I pursued in order to enable me to redeem my family. In the night time I fished with set-nets and pots for eels and lobsters, and shortly after went a whaling voyage in the service of Col. Smith.—After being out seven months, the vessel returned, laden with four hundred barrels of oil. About this time, I become possessed of another dwelling-house, and my temporal affairs were in a pretty prosperous condition. This and my industry was what alone saved me from being expelled that part of the island in which I resided, as an act was passed by the select-men of the place, that all negroes residing there should be expelled.

Sap Rising
(1773)

As soon as the peepers start their nightly song,
I set my nets across the swollen creek,
ready for the alewives' headlong run upstream.
For two weeks I'll sell herring by the wagonload,
and I'll salt a barrel away for future need.
If the run is good this year, I'll buy my wife
before she shows, and get a bonus child.
Hauling nets in, I notice again how birds
conduct conversations with others of their kind.
That grand old man in his black-and-white-checked coat
and jolly red cap must be making a speech
in woodpeckerish. Just listen to him tap!
What are they saying, Brother Woodpecker's drums?

> *(Tenderest tidings, potential future mate:*
> *I lack! Seek poke, titillation. Trust luck.)*

> ...

> *(Triplequick chick will trade tricky tickles!)*

Hmmm. Must be a she-pecker tapping her answer back.
Some hollow tree trunk is about to become a home.
Another good haul, and this child will be born free.

Next after my wife, I purchased a negro man for four hundred dollars. But he having an inclination to return to his old master, I therefore let him go. Shortly after I purchased another negro man for twenty-five pounds, whom I parted with shortly after.

Being about forty-six years old, I bought my oldest child Hannah, of Ray Mumford, for forty-four pounds, and she still resided with him. I had already redeemed from slavery, myself, my wife and three children, besides three negro men.

About the forty-seventh year of my life, I disposed of all my property at Long-Island, and came from thence into East-Haddam: I hired myself out at first to Timothy Chapman, for five weeks, the earnings of which time I put up carefully by me. After this I wrought for Abel Bingham about six weeks. I then put my money together and purchased of said Bingham ten acres of land, lying at Haddam neck, where I now reside.—On this land I labored with great diligence for two years, and shortly after purchased six acres more of land contiguous to my other. One year from that time I purchased seventy acres more of the same man, and paid for it mostly with the produce of my other land. Soon after I bought this last lot of land, I set up a comfortable dwelling house on my farm, and built it from the produce thereof. Shortly after I had much trouble and expence with my daughter Hannah, whose name has before been mentioned in this account. She was married soon after I redeemed her, to one Isaac, a free negro, and shortly after her marriage fell sick of a mortal disease; her husband a dissolute and abandoned wretch, paid but little attention to her in her illness. I therefore thought it best to bring her to my house and nurse her there. I procured her

Farm Garden

(ca. 1780)

By the time I was thirty-six I had been sold
three times. I had spun money out of sweat.
I'd been cheated and beaten. I had paid an enormous sum
for my freedom. And ten years farther on I've come
out here to my garden at the first faint hint of light
to inventory the riches I now hold.

My potatoes look fine, and my corn, my squash, my beans.
My tobacco is strutting, spreading its velvety wings.
My cabbages are almost as big as my head.
From labor and luck I have much profited.
I wish I could remember those praise-songs
we used to dance to, with the sacred drums.

My rooster is calling my hens from my stone wall.
In my meadow, my horses and my cows look up,
then graze again. My orchard boasts green fruit.
Yes, everything I own is dearly bought,
but gratitude is a never-emptying cup,
my life equal measures pain and windfall.

My effigies to scare raccoons and crows
frown fiercely, wearing a clattering fringe of shells,
like dancers in the *whatdidwecallit?* dance.
My wife and two of my children stir in my house.
For one thirty years enslaved, I have done well.
I am free and clear; not one penny do I owe.

I own myself—a five-hundred-dollar man—
and two thousand dollars' worth of family.
Of canoes and boats, right now I own twenty-nine.
Seventy acres of bountiful land is mine.
God, or gods, thanks for raining these blessings on me.
I turn around slowly. I own everything I scan.

all the aid mortals could afford, but notwithstanding this she fell a prey to her disease, after a lingering and painful endurance of it.

The physician's bills for attending her during her illness amounted to forty pounds. Having reached my fifty-fourth year, a hired two negro men, one named William Jacklin, and the other Mingo. Mingo lived with me one year, and having received his wages, run in debt to me eight dollars, for which he gave me his note. Presently after he tried to run away from me without troubling himself to pay up his note. I procured a warrant, took him, and requested him to go to Justice Throop's of his own accord, but he refusing, I took him on my shoulders, and carried him there; distant about two miles. The justice asking me if I had my prisoner's note with me, and replying that I had not, he told me that I must return with him and get it. Accordingly I carried Mingo back on my shoulders, but before we arrived at my dwelling, he complained of being hurt, and asked me if this was not a hard way of treating our fellow creatures. I answered him that it would be hard thus to treat our honest fellow creatures. He then told me that if I would let him off my shoulders, he had a pair of silver shoe-buckles, one shirt and a pocket handkerchief, which he would turn out to me. I agreed, and let him return home with me on foot; but the very following night, he slipped from me, stole my horse and has never paid me even his note. The other negro man, Jacklin, being a comb-maker by trade, he requested me to set him up, and promised to reward me well with his labor. Accordingly I bought him a set of tools for making combs, and procured him stock. He worked at my house about one year, and then run away from me with all his combs, and owed me for all his board.

Mingo

(ca. 1784)

I hired Mingo for one year,
paid him an honest wage.
But he owed eight dollars he'd borrowed of me,
and he decided to run away. Mingo up and ran away.

He'd made his mark on a note I wrote—
I can write, though I cannot read—
and an honest man is as good as his word.
A man's word is a bond. Yes, a man's word is his bond.

I caught him, requested that Mingo come
with me to the magistrate.
But Mingo's response was so quarrelsome
that I became irate. I'll admit, I was irate.

Over my shoulders I slung him;
I carried him up the road.
Onto the floor I flung him.
Justice Throop listened to me explode. I surely did explode.

Throop asked if I'd brought Mingo's note.
No: I'd left it at home, in my chest.
There was nothing for me to do but tote
Mingo back, despite his protest. Tote him back, despite his protest.

Since my residence at Haddam neck, I have owned of boats, canoes and sail vessels, not less than twenty. These I mostly employed in the fishing and trafficking business, and in these occupations I have been cheated out of considerable money by people whom I traded with taking advantage of my ignorance of numbers.

About twelve years ago, I hired a whale-boat and four black men, and proceeded to Long-Island after a load of round clams. Having arrived there, I first purchased of James Webb, son of Orange Webb, six hundred and sixty clams, and afterwards, with the help of my men, finished loading my boat. The same evening, however, this Webb stole my boat, and went in her to Connecticut river, and sold her cargo for his own benefit. I thereupon pursued him, and at length, after an additional expence of nine crowns, recovered the boat; but for the proceeds of her cargo I never could obtain any compensation.

Four years after, I met with another loss, far superior to this in value, and I think by no less wicked means. Being going to New-London with a grand-child, I took passage in an Indian's boat, and went there with him. On our return, the Indian took on board two hogsheads of molasses, one of which belonged to Capt. Elisha Hart, of Saybrook, to be delivered on his wharf. When we arrived there, and while I was gone, at the request of the Indian, to inform Captain Hart of his arrival, and receive the freight for him, one hogshead of the molasses had been lost overboard by the people in attempting to land it on the wharf. Although I was absent at the time, and had no concern whatever in the business, as was known to a number of respectable witnesses, I was nevertheless prosecuted by this conscientious gentleman, (the Indian not being able to pay for it) and

He promised, if I would put him down,
all he owned in this earthly life:
the silver shoe buckles he wore in town,
one shirt, and a handkerchief. One shirt, and a handkerchief.

And that very night Mingo slipped from me,
stole my horse, and disappeared.
Only words: "promise," "slavery," "free."
But a man is as good as his word. Yes, a man is as true as his word.

obliged to pay upwards of ten pounds lawful money, with all the costs of court. I applied to several gentlemen for counsel in this affair, and they advised me, as my adversary was rich, and threatened to carry the matter from court to court till it would cost me more than the first damages would be to pay the sum and submit to the injury; which I according did, and he has often since insultingly taunted me with my unmerited misfortune. Such a proceeding as this, committed on a defenceless stranger, almost worn out in the hard service of the world, without any foundation in reason or justice, whatever it may be called in a christian land, would in my native country have been branded as a crime equal to highway robbery. But Captain Hart was a *white gentleman*, and I a *poor African*, therefore it was *all right, and good enough for the black dog.*

I am now sixty nine years old. Though once strait and tall, measuring without shoes six feet one inch and an half, and every way well proportioned, I am now bowed down with age and hardship. My strength which was once equal if not superior to any man whom I have ever seen, is now enfeebled so that life is a burden, and it is with fatigue that I can walk a couple of miles, stooping over my staff. Other griefs are still behind, on account of which some aged people, at least, will pity me. My eye-sight has gradually failed, till I am almost blind, and whenever I go abroad one of my grand-children must direct my way; besides for many years I have been much pained and troubled with an ulcer on one of my legs. But amidst all my griefs and pains, I have many consolations; Meg, the wife of my youth, whom I married for love, and bought with my money, is still alive. My freedom is a privilege which nothing else can equal. Notwithstanding all the losses I have suffered by fire, by

The Incident of the Clams

(ca. 1785)

White sailors seem to think blacks should not sail,
except as muscle under white employ.
They think they own the sea, too, and the gale.
I've seen whole crews spit when I called *Ahoy*.
Some will stop at nothing to sink a black man's plans.
For instance, last week's incident of the clams.

I had hired a whaler and a crew of four,
and purchased six hundred sixty at Montauk
from James Webb, son of Orange Webb. A more
despicable white lowlife never walked
the earth. Hearing what my profit would be
in Connecticut, Webb stole the boat from me
and sold my clams in Middletown for his
own benefit. I did recover the boat
but was never compensated for my loss.
Thus, purchase, rent, and wages went for naught.
No recourse, no justice for the African
taunted with insult on sea as on land.

But, skimming toward haven under the evening star,
a man is just a man looking toward home.
The sea don't give a whit what color you are.
The constant stars know everyone by name.
I was *Broteer* once. Then I was a slave.
Who is this, giving my thanks for being alive?

the injustice of knaves, by the cruelty and oppression of false hearted friends, and the perfidy of my own countrymen whom I have assisted and redeemed from bondage, I am now possessed of more than one hundred acres of land, and three habitable dwelling houses. It gives me joy to think that I *have* and that I *deserve* so good a character, especially for *truth* and *integrity*. While I am now looking to the grave as my home, my joy for this world would be full—IF my children, Cuff for whom I paid two hundred dollars when a boy, and Solomon who was born soon after I purchased his mother—If Cuff and Solomon—O! that they had walked in the way of their father. But a father's lips are closed in silence and in grief!—Vanity of vanities, all is vanity!

Finis

The Freedom Business

(ca. 1790)

Freeing people is good business, in principle.
You'd think they'd thank you for sixty percent
of their earnings while they repay your capital
investment: business and benevolence,
for once, going hand in hand. But people think
your freeing them means they are free to leave
or lollygag. And your money, carefully banked,
then paid to The Man out of brotherly love,
might as well be tossed down the privy hole.

The first person I freed cost sixty pounds,
and had repaid twenty when the fellow stole
away by night. The second turned around
and went back to his master, so I lost
four hundred dollars for nothing. And the third
and I simply decided it was best
to part company. Frankly, the reward
for freeing people is a broken heart.

My son Solomon (seventy-five pounds)
sent on a whaler, his young life cut short
by scurvy. My daughter (forty-four pounds)
marrying a fool and contracting a fatal disease.
I paid for a physician (forty pounds),
but Hannah died. God has mysterious ways.
And freedom is definitely not a matter of funds.
Freedom's a matter of making history,
of venturing forth toward a time when freedom is free.

Certificate

STONINGTON, November 3, 1793.

THESE certify, that VENTURE, a free negro man, aged about 69 years, and was, as we have ever understood, a native of Africa, and formerly a slave to Mr. James Mumford, of Fisher's-Island, in the state of New-York; who sold him to Mr. Thomas Stanton, 2d, of Stonington, in the state of Connecticut, and said Stanton sold said VENTURE to Col. Oliver Smith, of the aforesaid place. That said VENTURE hath sustained the character of a faithful servant, and that of a temperate, honest and industrious man, and being ever intent on obtaining his freedom, he was indulged by his masters after the ordinary labour on the days of his servitude, to improve the nights in fishing and other employments to his own emolument, in which time he procured so much money as to purchase his freedom from his late master Col. Smith; after which he took upon himself the name of VENTURE SMITH, and has since his freedom purchased a negro woman, called Meg, to whom he was previously married, and also his children who were slaves, and said VENTURE has since removed himself and family to the town of East-Haddam, in this state, where he hath purchased lands on which he hath built a house, and there taken up his abode.

NATHANIEL MINOR, Esq.
ELIJAH PALMER, Esq.
Capt. AMOS PALMER,
ACORS SHEFFIELD,
EDWARD SMITH.

A Note on the Art

In creating artwork for *The Freedom Business*, my main goal was not to illustrate the narrative or the poems but to create images that continue on the path of reawakening this eighteenth-century story. Marilyn's poems extract her emotional response to Venture's compelling narrative. With both of these as my starting point, my artwork is an extension of my response to these poems. I highlighted specific lines or phrases in each poem that were compelling to me. My reading and rereading of them allowed them to resonate within me and helped me capture that intentionally poignant moment or element as a companion to the poem.

In "Pestilence," my visceral response to the lines "Slavery's wide wings gliding overhead / spread an infecting shadow as, step by step, / they swept like a battalion of ravenous ants, / advancing through the landscape ..." was to use a variety of bamboo pens and sticks dipped in ink to create a funnel cloud of multiple broken lines.

All of the paintings were created using a combination of watercolor, ink, collage, and acrylic paint in a process that was designed to create visual metaphors to the poems. The palette of ochre, sepia, blues, and greenish grays was used to evoke moods, earth tones, skin, water, vegetation, and atmosphere—all sensate colors that floated through my mind as I read the poems.

—*Deborah Dancy*

Acknowledgments

Few copies of the 1798 edition of the narrative of Venture Smith remain. We wish to thank Connecticut College, which owns this copy, and the University Library of the University of North Carolina, Chapel Hill, which transcribed this document as part of its digital publishing initiative, Documenting the American South, for permission to use this narrative. We are also grateful to the Florence Griswold Museum for permission to reproduce Paul Mutino's photograph of the narrative's title page.

I would like to thank Jeff Anderson, Anne Farrow, Abraham Abdul Haqq, Darin Keech, David Rau, Chandler B. Saint, Robert Tilton, and the seventh, eighth, and ninth generations of Venture Smith/Broteer Furro's descendants, who guided, encouraged, and inspired my work.
—*M.N.*